Loving a Fragile Woman

Samuel Tolbert

Table of Contents

Dedication

I first dedicate this book to God, the Creator of the universe, maker of Heaven and Earth. He has given me the words to share my experience. He has inspired every word and punctuation in this book. I believe no words will be wasted. I also dedicate this book to my beautiful wife, Tre'elle Tolbert. She has taught me so much while on this journey.

Words can't express how much I appreciate you. This is our new beginning and I wouldn't choose any other person to share this story with. I love you so much. Finally, I dedicate this book to my beautiful children Samuel Tolbert Jr. (SJ), Kristen Tolbert, Noelle Tolbert, and Noah Tolbert. I hope this book impact your lives greatly, in a positive way. I love you all to life.

Introduction

I believe women are very strong and unique. Especially the one's who actually embrace their inner strength. That's another lesson for another day. Growing up I saw how my mother took care of the household. I personally believe she has done everything in her strength and power to make sure all of us were taken care of. What I can say is, she's a strong woman (insert smile). While I first experienced the strength of a woman through my mother, I didn't fully understand that strength until I married my beautiful best friend. I've seen just how strong they really are through my wife.

Women have the ability to physically carry the very thing that helps keep this world from falling apart, which is life. While God has given women the strength to carry something so precious and valuable, there are things some women experience in life, which

sometimes causes them to abort life before it begins.

No, I'm not referring to natural abortion; I'm talking

about aborting the purpose God planted inside of you.

The seed that is designed to collide with your destiny,

causing everything that was intended for you to

manifest in your life.

As a matter of fact, this is the reason why the enemy

attacks women when their young. If he can kill purpose

before you come into the revelation of your identity, he

potentially kills every nation that you're designed to give

birth to. This is the abortion I'm talking about.

I don't want to ignore the fact that some of our women

have experienced sexual trauma that now prevents them

from being able to physically carry life. This in itself

upsets me thinking about it. To be honest, that's an

entire book by itself. While there are so many different

types of trauma someone can experience, I believe physical abuse could very well have a two-fold effect. Someone who faced this type of abuse could experience either psychological damage or physical damage.

From physical to verbal abuse, these things can really have a damaging effect on anybody experiencing such traumas. I would like to focus on the fragileness of some of our women, as it relates to them having to live through wholeness. I'm not talking about a physical weakness, but rather psychological pain many have suffered in their childhood and in some instances, adulthood. My hope is to bring you a new perspective of how to love a fragile woman. I'm aware that we all handle trauma differently. The way I navigate in my marriage is tailored to how I understand my wife. How I understand her deepest pain.

This book is designed to open your mind. Hopefully, at the conclusion of this book, you will have looked internally at yourself. Truth is, you can't help someone walk in wholeness if you fail to acknowledge your own brokenness. Throughout this book, I will reveal to you some of my struggles as a husband and also, some of the challenges my wife and I had to face together. You will begin to see how important honesty is in a marriage. Some of those hard topics you really don't want to discuss are usually the ones that can help pull you and your spouse through deliverance and freedom.

As you will see from my experience, it's not easy. I personally had to make up in my mind, that I wanted to see my wife healed and walking in wholeness. I'm not talking about being healed from physical sickness. The truth is my wife was psychologically broken. She was fragile.

There was so much she experienced in her life, which brought her to a place of uncertainty, disappointment, fear, anxiety, self-hate, and more. God decided to use and work through me, to help bring her through deliverance. Bring her into complete wholeness. But, why me?

I know I'm not the only one who has asked this question before. Some of you are probably still asking yourself that question. Let me help you. Why not you? I wasn't sure if I was qualified or not. I was still dealing with my own internal issues at the time. I had just gotten out of a relationship that left me questioning so much. There was internal healing and deliverance I had to get through. How in the world was I supposed to help someone fight, while at the same time working to keep my sanity? The thing about it, I wasn't in a good place when I met my wife, and she really had no idea. I will share that journey with you in another book of mine.

Some of you are probably asking what does this have to do with loving a fragile woman? Everything! Let's be honest, how can you help someone heal but you're still fighting for your life? How can you love someone properly if you're still trying to understand what is real love? When I met my wife, I was mentally in a bad place. I was broken too. You mean to tell me God had a plan to use two broken people to bring healing to a broken world? Do you know how powerful this is?

I know some of you who are reading this are probably trying to make sense of your life. Why did God allow me to go through so much? Where was God when I needed Him the most? Let me help you, some things we will never fully understand. But one thing I do know is, God finds a way to get the glory out of some of the messiest situations. Don't get me wrong. I know this is easier said than seen and understood.

I had to learn that in order for God to use me beyond my maximum capacity, I had to give everything I was and everything I am to Him. I had to even give Him my deepest hurt and pain. Understand, the moment you give up control is the moment God begins to use those broken pieces to produce Glory out of it. This is important on so many levels. If I wanted to see my wife walk in complete wholeness, I couldn't allow my brokenness to determine how I handled her. I had to handle her with care.

I'm sure you all are familiar with the symbol that is seen on a delivered package. The symbol of what appears to be a broken glass. This is a warning to let you know that something fragile is in the package and to handle with care. My wife was fragile and there were so many warnings to let me know that I couldn't handle her like any other relationships in my past. I had to learn how to treat her as she walks into wholeness.

The statement is true, "broken people do broken things". In other words, if I didn't take my healing and deliverance seriously, I could've potentially pushed my wife further into a dark place. The fact is I had to heal too. I didn't want this book to highlight the brokenness of my wife and not expose my internal battle in the mind. If you thought I was going to give you this three-step plan to understanding a fragile woman, you're wrong. In fact, how can you try to understand someone else, if you don't even understand yourself? I had to learn that in order for me to help my wife heal, I had to face myself. I had to ask God to show me who I was.

During those times, I had to really seek God for my life. I would ask the question "Who am I?" I realized my pains didn't define who I was, and the people around me certainly didn't define who God designed me to be. Men, this is very important. If you really want to help your wife heal, find your identity. She needs you to be who God called you to be. Know and be confident in the fact that your identity is only found in Him. When you step into the revelation of who He is in your life, God will reveal to you who He made you to be. He will also allow you to see a glimpse of where He's taking you. There's power and authority in knowing who you are.

I had to really become confident in my identity. While He was showing me who I am, He was also preparing me for my wife. My wife was damaged. I didn't know how fragile she was until she began to open up to me. Once my wife and I got married, that wasn't the time for me to start going through an identity crisis. In order to understand how to love a fragile woman, I had to be certain in who I was.

Many of our women have gone through so much pain in their life. Some in which carry that hurt for years, failing to fully heal and recover. It has even caused them to become fragile and often broken. The thing about it, what you often see on the outside is different from who they are on the inside. We tend to fall in love with what a woman projects to be, you know, the makeup and the laid hair. We even fall in love with their success. You have no idea what she's battling within her mind. Unfortunately, we as men can be so disconnected that we miss her silent cries. Later on, I will explain exactly what I'm talking about.

In today's world, I can only imagine how difficult it is finding someone who loves you for who you are. That is someone who not only loves the pleasant things about you but who could also have patience with you while you're seeking wholeness. Outside of physical appearances, there's an emotional side we often ignore. You're usually not aware of the traumatic experiences someone has gone through until that individual begins speaking or crying out from an emotionally shattered place. At that point, you can no longer ignore those signs of brokenness. You then must deal with it.

My wife told me how she would tell men who were interested in her, "You can't handle me". Crazy thing about it, they all thought she was speaking of whether or not they could handle her in bed. The truth is, my wife was fragile when I met her. Now, I didn't know how badly my wife was hurting at the time. I would later find out that I had to handle her in a special way. Through experience, I personally had to become the emotional support for my wife, as we both journeyed the road to wholeness.

Throughout this book, I share my approach to loving a fragile woman. I provide insight on ways of recognizing and understanding a woman's deepest pain. I also open up to you, by explaining some of the challenges my wife and I faced in our marriage. The fact is, my wife was damaged and needed someone who could handle her with care. In addition to my wife's brokenness, I was also dealing with my own issues. Truth is I had skeletons I had to expose and release. This was the only way I could assist my wife with her healing process.

I didn't know how vital my role would be as her husband until she began to fully trust and open herself up to me. She started showing me what her heart really looked like. The secrets she held on to for years, was like cancer. It was slowly killing her. Once we got married, I didn't know how powerfully God was going to use me to help her walk through wholeness. Because she was broken, I was willing to do anything to see her live in total freedom. We had to heal together.

Chapter 1
"I do!"

My wife and I have been married now for eight years, with four beautiful children. Our oldest son Samuel Jr. "SJ" is six years old. Our oldest daughter, Kristen is five years old. And we have a three-year-old set of twins, boy and girl whose names are Noah and Noelle. These kids are our life! My wife and I will do whatever it takes to protect them.

Let's be honest, we live in a ruthless world. You don't want to imagine anybody taking advantage of your children. God forbid you find out someone has tried to touch them inappropriately. Unfortunately, this is the world we live in, a world of selfish and greedy individuals who only care about the fulfillment of their own desires. At the end of the day, my wife and I vow to be there for our children physically, emotionally but most of all spiritually.

It's amazing how I can look at our children and see some of the same characteristics my wife and I show in them. Outside of looks, I can see a resemblance in their actions that reflect ours as well. For example, our daughter Kristen is so dope. She puts me in the mind of her mother. Through Kristen, I can see the potential my wife had when she was my daughters' age. From the high energy to the creativity, you can see they both have bright futures.

I believe as parents, we play a major role in how our children perceive the world. We have the opportunity to really become that example to them. My wife and I often encourage them to talk to us. We want to know what's going on in their tiny minds. One of the worse things that can happen is, your kids become too afraid to open up to you. I'm not saying you should become their best friend. At the end of the day, I believe there should be a boundary. It's up to you to find out what works for you and your household. Either way, open communication between you and your children is important. You will find out why later on.

My wife and I had to understand that if we didn't deal with our skeletons or traumas, we could potentially allow what we've dealt with in the past to pass through to our children. We had to learn that there's a danger in holding on to family secrets. I'm not talking about your family's secret recipe for peach cobbler. I'm referring to the physical and verbal abuse that happens behind closed doors. Sometimes, when you don't expose it, you begin to see the manifestation in your kids. This is how generational cycles are passed down through your bloodline.

My wife and I have had many ups and downs during the course of building something so powerful. On the outside looking at our marriage, it appeared we had it all together. In fact, whenever we would post a video or picture on social media, we often see people leave comments such as "marriage goals". I wish I had the confidence to reply, "are you sure?" The reality was, we were in a serious process to wholeness.

I believe it's okay to admire other marriages. It gives you something to look forward to. It allows you to live in hope, believing that one day you will find that perfect someone. That person was designed just for you. This is actually true. There's a soul mate God made for you. Someone you can love and spend the rest of your life with. Not to be limited to married peoples responsibilities, but to also be able to handle each other's darkest secrets.

Prior to marriage, my wife and I shared some painful things with each other. Once we entered into marriage, we then had to learn how to not only cope with the brokenness but also heal from the memories of trauma. This is a daily task for us. No days off! The question is how bad do you want to make it to wholeness? If you want it bad enough, you're willing to do whatever it takes. This comes at the cost of being selfless. If you're selfish, this journey isn't for you.

The truth is we're literally learning something new about each other every day. I personally believe that as long as you are breathing, you will always discover something new about your significant other. Things you've never known before, secrets that could bring you to your knees. When you say "I do", you're not only saying "I do" in response to the vows, but you're also making that commitment to marry even her deepest pains. That means you now have to heal with her! I know this to be true because the moment my wife shared with me what happened to her, it shifted my entire life.

When my wife and I were standing at the altar on our wedding day, we had no idea what was really happening emotionally. While we were coming together as one, there was also a merger of the heart happening. The eloquent decorations at our wedding may have looked appealing to the naked eye, it didn't reflect what our heart looked like. We were two broken people coming together. Someone might ask why would two people enter a marriage broken? I personally believe we often marry someone, hoping it would expedite our healing process. If I marry him or her, it will fill that empty void. The truth is, wholeness can't be rushed. I wasn't thinking on this level at the time. My wife and I were ready to marry each other and there was nothing anybody could do or say about it.

My wife and I decided to say our own marriage vows on our wedding day. Prior to sharing those vows with each other, the pastor read the traditional vows to us. Some of you may be familiar with "for better, for worse, for richer, for poorer, in sickness and in health, till death do us part". This might not be verbatim but you get it.

If I can be honest, at the beginning of our marriage, my wife and I had to face the "sickness and in health" part of the vows. Psychologically my wife was broken. Her heart was fragile. She wasn't well. But for better and for worse, I was willing to fight with her. This marriage vow wasn't limited to physical sickness or a medical condition. Mentally my wife was sinking into a dark place. While she shared her secrets with me prior to marriage, once we got married, it wasn't enough to only have knowledge of her trauma. When I vowed "Until death do us part", and "In sickness and in health", I also made a life long commitment to heal with her.

My wife is so dope and unique. While the uniqueness of a person can be so attractive, what about the hidden emotions many of us don't want to deal with? That inner person we often ignore, blinded by the external success and accomplishments. While those things are great, it means nothing if you're plummeting away internally. In my wife's book "Walking In Wholeness", she explains why she put so much energy into becoming successful. What was the driving force behind of her accomplishments?

There was a reason why my wife made a push to further her education. She was always motivated to being number one in everything she put her mind to. It was as if she had so much to prove. Who was she trying to prove herself to and why? She was broken and if anyone paid attention, you could see it in how bad she wanted to be successful. My wife's book explains this well. I really had to learn how to look beyond the outward shell of my wife, and look at what was happening inwardly. My wife was sinking, and I had to learn how to love a fragile woman.

Prior to marriage, I had an idea of what marriage looked like. Well, at least I thought I did. While I knew the characteristics of a healthy marriage before entering a life long commitment, I still had to learn how to be a husband to my wife. Understand, when two people come together, you're now a part of everything they are. The more you get to know your spouse, the more you also learn about yourself. Trust me, I've spent many days and nights examining everything marriage has taught me. If I can give you some advice, listen to the non-verbal language of your spouse. Later on in this book, we will dive deeper into what I'm talking about.

Let me back up just a little. Before we both said, "I do", we developed a dope friendship. We genuinely just enjoyed each other's company. The first time I saw her we were both enlisted in the Navy on the same ship. I remember us being on a working party, in the middle of the ocean. I made eye contact with her. Well, at least I thought she was looking at me. She was really looking at this dark-skinned guy standing behind me. That's beside the point. The thing is, I knew she wanted me. This is my story and I'm sticking to it!

Somehow, a conversation was initiated between us. I could tell she immediately felt comfortable around me.

For one, our last names were similar. My last name is Tolbert, while her last name was Talbert. Do you see the difference?

Once our ship pulled back into homeport, we stayed in touch with each other. She was so dope to be around. As I mentioned earlier, I was broken and I needed someone like her to take my mind off of my brokenness. We played basketball together. I ended up winning every single game. I'm sure her story is different from mine.

Music was one of the things that allowed us to keep each other's attention. She played the guitar, the keyboard, and the clarinet, while my main focus was the keyboard. Long story short, we would go on unofficial dates to the Guitar Center. For some of my musicians who know, this is seriously the spot to be at. Because we're both into music, those moments were the perfect time to really get to know my best friend and build a bond outside of work.

I believe it's important for me to share how we met. At that time, we were both going through separate processes. We were both in a constant battle in our minds. There were things we've experienced, that really could have destroyed us mentally. We were in the middle of trying to find our identity. Remember I explained to you earlier that it was important for me to know my identity. The fact is I couldn't pursue a relationship if I didn't know who I was, especially with someone else who was so broken. I would've made a mess of everything. My wife needed someone who was at least trying to become whole.

While we were both on separate roads to healing, I remember times where my then best friend was crying out for help. I missed every sign! At the time, I knew we hadn't gotten to that point of fully opening up to each other about some of our deepest fears. Those painful experiences that pushed us into dark places.

Speaking of crying out, I remember a time we were at her place. She plugged up her small keyboard and began to play. She asked me to teach her how to play one of her favorite songs by Jill Scott "He Loves Me". She had just gotten out of the shower. As she's standing there in only a towel, I stayed focused on the task at hand, teach her how to play "He Loves Me".

Some may think this is an innocent moment, but I believe this was a time where she was crying out. I can only imagine the psychological battle she went through once I left her place. I'm sure she felt unwanted and rejected. I know she had questions. I really believe this experience was beginning to change her perspective of men. At the end of the day, her greatest hurt and pain came by the hands of the men she once trusted in her life. She was crying out from a dark place but I missed the signs.

Why am I telling you all of this? I'm glad you asked! When my wife and I got married, she brought up this moment. She told me that the reason why she came out in only a towel was to see how I would respond. She wanted to know if I was interested in her or not. She went on to tell me that the only way she knew a guy liked her was if they tried to come on to her sexually. Well, my response threw her off. I personally had way too much respect for her. Besides, I was still healing and I really didn't want to ruin a perfect friendship. I believe many people often make the mistake of hopping into a relationship in denial. The truth is, you're broken and you hope no one unveils your damaged heart. I promise you it takes the right person that can handle everything you are.

She went on to explain to me how she likes having control. Had I responded in a way that was familiar to her, it would have fed her intentions of controlling every possible outcome in her life. My wife was big on keeping her numbers low and not letting it go up. This number was referring to the number of men she allowed in. This was her way of controlling that part of her life.

Whenever you pursue someone you're interested in, more than likely you're not going to disclose your darkest secrets from the jump. Matter of fact, you will enter that relationship, presenting to them the image of wholeness. The truth is, you're broken and you only hope the individual you're dealing with doesn't see the hidden pain you're experiencing. There's a danger in presenting a false image of who you are. That image may work for a season, but eventually, the underlining issues become exposed. Those darkest secrets are revealed through your actions. You begin speaking out from your brokenness.

This is why I believe effective premarital counseling is so important. You get a chance to understand the person you're about to spend the rest of your life with. While this is ideal, unfortunately, this is not realistic. You typically don't pursue someone because of the things that are not seen, it's usually because of what is presented to you, a person's external image.

I believe damaged people tend to hurt other people, especially if they're not honest with themselves. You will see what I mean by this later on in this book. I would say transparency is important when trying to reach that level of wholeness. My wife and I really had to become transparent with each other. Once my wife started revealing her darkest secrets to me, I was then able to help her navigate her emotions. I couldn't navigate what I couldn't see. This is where open communication comes into play. We all can agree that communication is the key to creating a healthy marriage. It's also vital when the two of you start seeking healing and wholeness.

Contrary to what some may believe, all marriages aren't the same. Just as each and every last one of us are designed differently, men should handle and treat their wife in such a way that is tailored to her personality, character, but most of all, her traumas. Please don't get freaked out by the word, "trauma". While many of us may not have a psychology degree, we still have the responsibility as the husband to learn and understand things such as, what triggers painful memories in your wife, and how to make adjustments in your marriage, so that you won't potentially lose her.

If I can make this claim, I honestly feel that in marriage, the love a husband has towards his wife should reflect how God loves us all daily. Ephesians 5:25 tell us "husbands love your wives, even as Christ loved the church". I had to understand that with God being all things to us, I had to become all things to my wife. I became a friend, a teacher, a father, and even a counselor. While I may not have the "credentials" of a counselor, the moment I said "I do", I took on that responsibility. I had to become a listening ear. If I didn't know the answer to all of her concerns, I still provided emotional support for her.

Let me be clear. I am an advocate of therapy. I believe there's nothing wrong with seeking professional help. However, as the husband, you have the opportunity to know the deepest parts of your wife. You get a chance to know her on a level counseling might not be able to reach. This makes sense because you're around your spouse more frequently than you would attend counseling sessions.

I had to even get to know my wife on levels that went beyond sex in the bedroom. I don't care how great you think you are in bed, there's an emotional spot you will never reach unless she let you in. That's where her deepest pains are. Some of the most painful memories are there. Once my wife and I got married, I began to see my wife's brokenness surface even during intimate moments.

To be honest, I believe there are many women waiting for their husbands to rescue them from a dark place of imprisonment. That emotional place is filled with anger, resentment, abandonment, fear, and even disappointment. Later on, I discuss a mental prison and how it affects a marriage.

There's a list of traits I consider common for a healthy marriage. These qualities include love, honesty, communication, trust, and commitment. While the common characteristics of a healthy marriage play a major role in the growth of a successful marriage, unfortunately, it's not enough. When you begin to explore and become aware of hidden pains and brokenness in a woman, you then see how the known characteristics only scratch the surface of real marriage. You begin to see how your "I do" seriously become a heavy responsibility. I would soon find out that there's more to marriage than what is seen on television, social media, and even in my household as a child.

I went into marriage thinking I knew what it took to be the best husband on the planet. I was fortunate to have had my mother and father around growing up. They are both God-fearing, which I believe is necessary when building a healthy marriage. I would watch how my father catered to the needs of the family. He assisted my mother in making sure we were all taken care of. From ensuring bills were paid, to even cooking whole meals for all 16 of us if necessary. Yes! I grew up with 14 siblings. That's another topic for another day.

My father knew how to fulfill his roles and responsibilities as the man of his household. While I remember how my parents treated each other and also how they loved on us, it still wasn't enough to prepare me for what I had to face in my marriage.

It wasn't until I got married where I found out that it was more to marriage than just providing a roof over my family's head and making sure they had food to eat. While being the provider is a major role of a man, there were internal issues my wife and I had to deal with together. some traumas happened during childhood.

There were also hidden pains we had to face and walkthrough.

To be completely honest, I spent a lot of time trying to figure out what was I doing wrong in my marriage. Why did my wife sometimes respond in a way of feeling uncomfortable when I would touch her a certain type of way? It was as if she would shut down completely. Was I losing my wife or was I thinking too much into it? These were some of the toughest moments of my life, wondering if I were doing my job as a husband. After all, I thought I had the whole marriage thing figured out. I found out that if those internal issues weren't handled, I could potentially lose her.

Chapter 2

"Mental Prison"

Whenever you meet a woman for the first time, you notice her smile, beauty, and even her curves. These characteristics are considered the shell of a woman. While it's so easy to draw your attention to these things, you must intentionally look beyond what is seen with the naked eye. You do this by having those deep conversations with each other, those talks that reveal traumas. Whenever my wife and I would sit and talk, I began to feel her emotions as she shared her hidden pains with me.

At this moment, I'm looking beyond the shell of my wife. I'm getting to know the "real" her, the broken her. I began to pay attention to her. What is her character like? Why does she respond in a certain type of way? What conversations tend to send her into a place she tries to avoid. What actions push her further into that mental prison?

Believe it or not, sometimes what a person reveals on the outside is contrary to what he or she feels internally. Whenever you meet someone for the very first time, you may not physically see the evidence of someone's emotional pain. Let's be honest, people don't just go around revealing their scars. Whenever someone experiences something so traumatic or hurtful in life, as a defense mechanism, walls are built. These walls also become what I call a mental prison. That's why it can sometimes take a little more time to understand a person who experienced trauma in their life. There's so much you have to fight through. Honestly, my fight didn't begin until my wife and I got married. My wife was confined to this mental cage. She wanted to be free but it was so much pushing against her freedom.

During the process of my wife's healing, I would often envision this little girl who was about ten years old. This girl would appear to be sitting in a cage, waiting for someone to rescue her. I remember telling my wife one day that I saw her as a little girl in a cage. It looked like she was being held against her will. I explained to my wife, the details I saw. For example, this little girl had ponytails, sitting in a corner of the cell. The crazy thing about it, my wife would tell me of accounts she also had of seeing herself in a prison.

I believe this vision was indeed showing us the mental state of my wife. Truthfully, while she seemed to be lonely in that prison, this was the place where she also felt safe from the world. She was hurt or dropped by many people that she had to build up these prison walls of the mind. She had become imprisoned by her own fears.

Let me explain what a physical prison is. These buildings are designed to legally hold people that have committed a crime. People who break the law are held there until they complete their sentence. From experience, I use to work at a prison as a correctional officer. It's nothing like what you see in movies. I had the opportunity to speak to some of the younger inmates during my shift. I would ask some of them what did they do to get in there. Now, I could've easily gone into the system to look it up, but I wanted to open up a dialogue.

What I noticed about some of their responses was, a lot of them admitted to being in the wrong place at the wrong time. Some of the inmates went on to say, they didn't want to snitch, so they decided to stay silent. Staying silent has cost some of them five, ten, or even fifteen years of their life. Isolated from the world. Being controlled by the systems set in place inside the prison. Having to be told what to do and when to do it. They didn't have the freedom to move like they wanted to move. There were restrictions. There were limitations.

Just like a physical prison, mental prisons have similar characteristics. Instead of being controlled by a manmade system that's put in place, you are controlled by fear. Fear tells you how to move and when to move. Fear causes you to push the right people out of your life while holding on to people that look familiar. You even become too afraid to speak. You decide it's easier to just keep it to yourself. While the individuals who hurt you appear to be free or unbothered, you're now being tormented by the secrets of your past. The very thoughts of the pain end up pushing you further into isolation. You then begin to find comfort in your brokenness. This mental prison has now become your reality.

At many of the prisons, you are no longer identified by your name. You're usually assigned a number. That number now identifies you. I would even say that the prison you're in identifies you. Whenever someone experiences something traumatic in their life, they allow the pains from their brokenness to identify them. They no longer identify themselves as the person God called them to be but rather by the broken pieces in their life. To be honest, your true identity becomes locked up and you now project who and what the trauma in your life says you are. You're now identified by your brokenness. Your pain identifies you.

My wife struggled to find good within her. Although she projected who she wanted people to see, she also projected her hurt and pain onto others. This wasn't necessarily intentional. At the end of the day, she allowed her distorted identity to guide her decisions. I would even say some of her decisions were perverted in nature. My wife does a great job explaining perversion in her book "Walking In Wholeness".

If I could explain it briefly, perversion isn't limited to how you see things sexually. Perversion also happens whenever you see the opposite of who and what God called you to be. In other words, your identity then becomes distorted. You no longer see any good within yourself. You also fail to see good in others around you. You begin to feel worthless. You don't know if you have a real purpose in life anymore, especially when you feel your purity has been taken from.

This is what a mental prison does to people who experienced trauma in their life. You start to approach every situation with a negative outlook. You must break free from your broken mind. Break free from the painful thoughts of your past. Begin to see yourself as God sees you. Look through the lens of promise and purpose. Ask God to reveal to you how He sees you as.

The main difference between a mental prison and a physical prison is after you do your time given to you in an actual prison, you are free to return into the community as a citizen. When it comes to mental isolation, you remain a prisoner to your mind, until you free yourself. Typically, this starts by being honest with yourself and exposing the person that hurt you. But then again, that's just the beginning. There is without question a process you have to go through. My wife explains this process in her story.

I can remember the moment my wife made up in her mind that she was going to expose the people who hurt her. She was carrying the pains of her secret for over twenty years. I know she was tired and was ready to live her life in wholeness. The start of her freedom I believe began the moment she became honest with herself. She knew she wasn't well. She felt trapped in her mind. She had become a prisoner of the painful thoughts of her past. Fear was killing her slowly. For the sake of her freedom, she decided it was time to expose it and release it. She also knew that if she hadn't exposed it, her children could've become the next target of sexual abuse.

As mentioned above in my conversation while working at the prison, some of the inmates didn't want to expose the people who really did the crime. To protect their family and friends they would rather take the fall. This is the same thing that happens in a mental prison. Some people become too afraid to tell the right people. They end up holding that painful secret for years. Some even fear that if they expose the individuals that caused the trauma, it could potentially bring shame or embarrassment to their family.

Do you know how much strength it took for my wife to open up to her family about her past? I'm sure this was one of the scariest things she had to do. What was my position and posture as she's doing something that would change the trajectory of our life? To be completely honest, I was as nervous as she was. But I knew I had to be there for her not only physically but also psychologically. I had to also be there for her spiritually. I was praying the entire time we were at her family's house.

I can remember the night my wife was about to expose her skeletons to her family. We were sitting in the room when all of a sudden she started to have a nervous breakdown. She was having another anxiety attack. We knew the time was approaching for her to expose her deepest pains. This moment was starting to put her in a place she really didn't want to be in. I was sitting there praying, while her friend was on the phone encouraging her, telling her that she can do this. My wife began to take deep breaths in order to calm down. Now she was ready to speak.

Understand this was still considered a mental prison for my wife. There were so many emotions running through her mind. I can only imagine what a returning citizen, someone who completed their time in prison feels when they're approaching that prison gate for the last time. That is the day they regain their freedom! They will never have to be confined to a prison cell again. This is a new beginning for them.

Just like that individual exiting a physical prison for the last time, whenever someone is experiencing psychological freedom, they now step into a new beginning of their life. Your perspective began to change. Instead of being identified by your brokenness, you now identify yourself by purpose. You began to embrace the identity God designed for you. You no longer allow the memories of those painful experiences to keep you imprisoned. Fear then becomes no more.

Mental prisons become a part of an individual's everyday life. As long as a woman stays within the walls, they feel safe and protected from the world. They feel protected from the types of people who hurt them. Women that build up walls due to past experiences are the only one who can knock down those walls surrounding her heart. This task isn't easy.

While God can do the miraculous in our lives overnight, there's a process to wholeness. While healing is our portion based on Isaiah 53:5 "By His stripes we are healed", wholeness becomes a process. My wife and I had to understand that the process of wholeness doesn't begin until you make up in our mind you want to be free. Once you make the effort of pursuing wholeness, then faith, patience, and the will to live is needed.

Chapter 3

"Can She Trust You?"

I believe there are parts of a woman's heart you will never reach unless she fully opens up and gives you access. That is where she has buried the pains and brokenness of her past. Believe it or not, there are some men that still struggle to understand the deepest parts of their wives. How can you possibly love a woman and not know and understand her deepest fears? While we're captivated by a woman's beauty and curves, there are some who are crying out from a deep place. This is where trust comes into play. Can she trust you?

What is love without trust? Can you truly love someone, while at the same time lack full trust in him or her? I personally believe someone's full trust must be earned. But what if you hop into a relationship with someone who lacks full trust in you? Not because of something you've done, but because of hurtful encounters with someone he or she use to trust.

While trust should be a foundational characteristic of a successful marriage or relationship, the reality is, it has to sometimes be earned. Let's be honest, we've all experienced a time where we lost trust in someone. Some of us have probably made the statement, "I don't trust nobody." At this point, as a defense mechanism, you have built up walls surrounding you and your brokenness. This wall is also known as a mental prison. Later on, I will talk more about the dangers of a mental prison. Meanwhile, let's discuss the importance of having trust in a marriage.

When I met my wife, I didn't know any of the traumas she had experienced. While it may have seemed she trusted me from the jump, that wasn't the case. My integrity had to be tested, and trust me it was. I remember the moment my wife decided to open up to me about her childhood trauma. The crazy thing about it, I actually had a dream that would soon reveal to me what happened to her as a child.

I had to learn that in order for me to fully understand my wife, I had to look past the exterior and see the innermost parts of her. These are the parts of her that she chooses to hide from the world, the scars and brokenness caused by traumatic experiences. My wife planned to remain a closed book until she found someone she trusted with her traumas. I had to establish a certain level of trust with her before we could begin the journey to wholeness.

One thing about it, trust wasn't given easily but I had to earn every ounce of it. A woman that has experienced so much hurt in her life will keep you at a distance until she's ready to move forward. I found out later on that this was her way of controlling the outcome of the situation. The wall my wife built up only allowed me to speak to her through the walls. Now, many of us make the mistake of giving up on someone that isn't moving at the pace we desire because we lack the patience to wait. I couldn't rush her. I really wanted my wife to heal and become whole properly. I was willing to wait for her.

Contrary to what some may believe, while trust is important at the beginning of a relationship, you may not experience a woman's full trust until three, four, five, or even seven years after the first date. Yes! This can really happen. I know we were taught that trust is the "foundation" of any relationship. While this is ideal, the reality is, when you pursue a woman who has experienced trauma from the people she loved, her full trust in you must be earned.

The keyword is "build". There's really no way around it. You have to build a level of trust with her and keep that trust. Especially when pursuing a fragile woman. Once again, you're now facing walls that were built because of traumatic experiences. There are many occurrences that can cause a woman to become fragile. Those things can range anywhere from verbal abuse to physical abuse.

I believe it's easy for a woman to hide her pains and traumas. Women can dress it up, put on makeup, and even pursue successful careers in order to hide their damaged hearts. My wife explains in her book "Walking Through Wholeness", how she would put so much energy in making sure she was number one in everything she did. Because of her painful experience, she became consumed in success. I later found out that this was only to mask her pain. Behind what you saw, a little girl who was crying out for help.

While there's nothing wrong with accomplishing whatever you set your mind to, you have to be careful not to be so focused on outward success that you start to suppress the inner hurt. As men, we have to be trusted enough for her to allow us to help her destroy the walls that trauma caused her to build. Truth is, it's not whether she can she trust you, but can she trust you with her brokenness? Yes, there's a difference. Can she trust you to cover her while she heals? Not only cover her physically but spiritually as well. This is important.

I found out that whenever a woman is going through their healing process, they become exposed. They become naked. I'm not talking about physical nakedness, but rather emotional vulnerability. Her scars are now being exposed. At this point, only clean hands and handle her. We can also look at this from a surgeon's perceptive. Whenever a doctor is prepping for a surgery, prior to the start of any procedure, he or she makes sure everything in that room is sterile. They want to ensure nothing harmful enters the patient during surgery.

This is why I asked the question "can she trust you?" Can she trust you to be in the operating room as she's going through her healing process? Can she trust that you won't allow anything harmful to infiltrate the sterile place she's in? These are questions I had to ask myself during my wife's journey to wholeness. I had to examine myself daily. I had to ask the Lord to examine my heart. Made sure my motives remained pure. Once again, I was committed to the process. I was not only committed, but I was also engaged with the process. In other words, I got involved with her restoration. I didn't just enter the room, and start touching things. I had to be patient. Yes, that word again. I had to make sure that none of my brokenness bled out onto her. I also had to put in work. This is what I'm talking about when I said I was also engaged in the process. Allow me to further explain.

When I partnered with my wife, I also partnered with her healing. I became all that her brokenness required in the moments. For example, my wife battled with rejection. This was also associated with the sexual traumas she experienced. The way I engaged with her brokenness was by making sure I was there when she needed me the most. I remember saying this in an earlier chapter, I had to become so much to her. It was my responsibility. The most important thing I became to her was a counselor. I had to take the time to know the insides of her, not sexually but her deepest emotional pains. I had to learn and listen to what her emotions were saying.

While my wife is lying on the operating table, I'm learning and understanding every part of her. First of all, I had to be trusted in the room before the process really began. Perhaps the reason why you're not seeing progress in the process is because you're not fully trusted by her. I would definitely begin to look inwardly at the things that could potentially cause her not to fully trust me. Ask yourself the question, "why hasn't she fully open up to me?" Is there something I'm doing that reminds her of her traumas? Trust me, if you really love her, you will do whatever it takes for her to reach that place of wholeness.

Speaking of earning her trust, our marriage had gotten interesting when we started having daughters. I'm sure you can imagine the mental state and the anxiety she was experiencing when we found out we were having our first daughter. While the excitement was there, fear also entered in. The questions began to pop up in my wife's mind such as, "What if he does what happened to me to our daughter?" Just typing this makes me sick to my stomach. I would never touch my daughters inappropriately, but the truth is my wife's truth or way of thinking was influenced by her traumas. Could my wife fully trust me around our princess? This is the question that constantly ran through my head.

I can remember times when my wife would stare at me while changing my daughter's diaper. This made me so uncomfortable to the point that I just stopped changing her altogether. I couldn't stand being watched like I was some random creepy man trying to look at our daughter's private parts. These moments were really beginning to break me. My mind was everywhere. The thoughts that were running through my wife's mind were very toxic on so many levels. How do I suppose to help my wife heal if she doesn't even trust me around our little girl?

To be honest, this went on for probably months. Come to think about it, I'm not sure if I ever changed my daughter again. This was around the time things were changing in our marriage. In a later chapter, I explain the changes that were happening. Truth is, there were times where our marriage was declining. I wasn't sure if there was any hope for us. I just wanted to be trusted. But the thing about it, I ended up doing something that really caused her not to trust me. I will discuss this later.

This is why I feel trust is so vital in a marriage, particularly when it comes to the two of you pursuing wholeness. I've said this before; it's impossible to walk in complete wholeness if your marriage lacks trust. One of the keys to healing is for the two of you to become

open, exposing your skeletons to each other. Once the

roots are exposed, you can then deal with the

underlining issues. Trust gives you the opportunity to

confront, confess, and release. You will see this again

later.

Chapter 4
"8853"

One evening, my wife who was then my best friend, decided to come to my apartment to take a nap. She was complaining about a serious headache she had. Let me insert here. Whenever my wife and I talk about this moment, we call it "8853". This was my apartment number. I promise you, I will never forget this day!

Now, while she was resting on the couch, and while I was playing NBA 2K, she experienced something that would change both of our lives. My eyes were locked on the TV screen, trying to score 80 points with my creative player. While I was extremely focused, there were spirits attacking or should I say tormenting her.

The way she explains it, she felt as though something was on top of her. It felt like a ton of bricks. She felt paralyzed and couldn't move nor could she speak. She told me she was yelling my name "Sam!" I heard nothing.

After she was finally able to move and speak, she asked, "Sam, you didn't hear me calling you?" I paused the game, and looked at her with a blank stare. I shook my head, "No". Now, what happened next changed the trajectory of our relationship. If I didn't know if demonic spirits were real, I would have definitely become a believer that night.

I moved over to the couch where she was now sitting. I began to look into her eyes. As I'm staring at her, it was as if I was looking into her soul. As I'm looking directly into her eyes, suddenly, the entire room got real dark.

At that moment, every hair on my body stood up. The look on my face and in my eyes was as if I saw a ghost.

She looked at me, as her eyes began to fill with water. She then asked me "What do you see?" Now, at that time, I was spiritual and had a relationship with God. I was actually an ordained minister. So, I knew what time it was. Understand, just because I knew what time it didn't necessarily mean I was ready to start casting out spirits. We were right in the middle of a demonic attack. But, why? What event led to this moment?

As I mentioned before, the entire room had gotten real dark. But the crazy thing about it, all the lights in my apartment were on. With a frighten look on her face, she asked me again, "What do you see?" Immediately God began speaking through me. I remember Him saying "There are doors that are open". Then, I responded to her and asked, "What are these doors?" I realized I was in a three-way conversation.

She looked at me and said, "I don't know", as she shook her head. I could tell this was the first time this ever happened to her. This is why it's important to be connected to someone who will help you unveil what's really happening internally. We had no idea this moment would happen but we knew it was a vital moment to begin the process of wholeness. Things were about to get interesting and she would soon after expose everything about her life. I seriously believe you can't release what you don't reveal.

What does this have to do with anything? A lot! This moment would be the beginning of my wife opening up to me concerning what happened to her as a child. She began to reveal her traumas with me, her darkest secrets. This was the beginning of her establishing trust with me. As stated before, trust is so vital for building any relationship. However, people who go through traumatic experiences don't easily give you their trust.

While trust should be the foundation of your marriage, I believe you may not have her full trust from the start. Some might ask, "Then why marry someone who doesn't fully trust you?" My response, there are painful experiences, disappointments, and brokenness that causes a woman not to fully trust anybody. So, I would say, don't take it personal. Now, that's not to say she doesn't love, this simply means, you have to earn that part of her heart. It takes someone who is willing to fight with her, be patient with her, and love on her.

Now, back to "8853". While we're still in that moment, and the room still seemed dark, I remember her telling me the age that it all started, to the age it all ended. The pain that gripped my heart when she said, "Sam, I was ten years old when it started". Listen, I didn't want to believe it at first. What she told me sent chills down my spin. I never told her this but I actually became very angry when she told me about her trauma. I felt fire moving through my bones and it wasn't the fire of God.

To be completely honest, in that moment I purposely suppressed my emotions surrounding what she told me. I actually bottled up my emotions for about seven years. She never really knew what was going on in my mind. Later on, after getting married, she explained to me why it was so important for me not to have shown emotions that night. It could've potentially caused her to shut down in that moment. She probably would've never opened up to me again concerning what she experienced as a child.

She went on to tell me of family members who tried to molest her when she was as young as five years old, but were unsuccessful. My wife carried the pains of her brokenness for over twenty years. I personally know women who had family members try to sexually assault them. They had to fight for their life. While fighting back protected some women from being penetrated, they still experienced psychological damage. This is trauma I wouldn't wish on nobody.

That night I remember calling a brother of mine asking him to pray for us. I felt we couldn't fight alone. I needed someone I could not only trust but also someone who I knew had a prayer life. We began to pray for the peace of God to enter my apartment. Notice I didn't try to cast out or expel any demons. To be honest, I didn't really feel qualified to do so. Clearly, we were dealing with demonic influences. After becoming married, my wife and I would, later on, become activated in deliverance and casting out unclean spirits. I will discuss more about spiritual warfare in a later chapter.

"8853" was a turning point for me. Prior to this moment, I never really confronted a demonic presence before, well at least not a manifested demon. Growing up in church, I've seen times where evil spirits would surface in people. I would hear people growling and acting out of character, but I was way too young to understand what was happening then. Although we didn't hear any sounds that night, there was still a silent cry for help. Every tear that rolled down her face was part of her story, the unspoken cry of her brokenness.

As we both sat on the couch in my apartment, trying to make sense of what just happened, God was establishing a new assignment inside of me. I was now aware of her trauma. From this point forward, God began to guide my every step while walking with my wife to wholeness.

I believe when you carry this type of pain and fail to fully heal from it, you eventually become angry and bitter. In some cases, you become upset with yourself, believing you're the one to blame for whatever happened to you in your past. My wife had to make it to that point of forgiving herself. Although she didn't do those things to herself, psychologically this was a major step towards healing and wholeness.

Chapter 5

"The Unspoken Language"

When my wife and I decided to take our relationship serious and get married, I begin to see underlining emotions surrounding her brokenness. Listen, sometimes my wife would snap on me out of nowhere. We could be having a good time one day, and all of a sudden, her mood changes. She would get very angry and upset. You all can imagine the energy that was in our home. It was pretty bad.

When this would happen, I already knew what time it was. Let me help the men. Anytime your wife's mood changes and it's not contributed to her monthly cycle, pay attention. This is what I call the hidden cry of her pain, the unspoken language. She could very well be crying out from a broken place. Her emotions could be everywhere at that time! Not because of something you've done wrong, but because she's trying to navigate her thoughts. Your wife could potentially be drowning in her emotions and you not even recognize it. Men, pay attention!

Unfortunately, we end up catching the heat of the battle in her mind. This is not the time for us as men to take it personal. You should make the necessary adjustments and help her navigate. Sometimes, just being present and not saying anything can help. What do I mean by "being present"? All of your focus needs to be on her in these moments. If your mind is on everything else but on what she's experiencing, you could very well miss signs of her sinking into a place of depression. Trust me, I was that guy! I would sometimes miss indications of my wife falling into a dark place.

I would have so many other things on my mind. Due to bills, and other responsibilities outside of our home, I would lose focus of what my wife was going through. She was really crying out! While she's sinking in her emotions, I'm thinking about my next move for the family. I believe there's nothing wrong with planning ahead for the sake of your household. I definitely encourage you to do so. However, you can't be so caught up on future planning, that you miss present moments of distress. I'm telling you from experience, your lack of focus as the man of your house could potentially destroy your family. You should make every effort to listen and really focus on the unspoken language of your wife. Men, get focused, and stay focused!

I had to learn the hard way. The atmosphere in my home was changing. It didn't help that I would come home, after working a twelve-hour shift and miss so many unspoken signs of depression. My wife was really sinking! She started experiencing anxiety. Her mind was so scattered. While I'm away, she was definitely being tormented by her past. I'm telling you all, sometimes I wasn't mentally present and I was hardly physically there for her. I knew it was a problem! Something had to change.

I remember a time I had to take my wife to the hospital. She wasn't feeling well at all. Once we got checked in and they called her back, the doctors began to go through their evaluations on her, you know, the checking of the weight and vitals. My vitals turned out to be normal. In between the nurses and doctors coming in and out of her room, she began having these episodes of anxiety. She literally felt like she was going to die. I would firmly grip her hand and tell her "you're going to be alright". I told her she was going to live because her family needed her. I also remember a random text from her friend coming in. She had no idea what my wife was experiencing at the time. The text read, "Keep fighting".

My wife seriously looked like she was about to die. She was taking these shallow breaths. As she gasps for air, I pressed the button that would signal the nurses at their station. My wife's nurse came in the room to see about her. She began to complain that she couldn't breathe. As I looked at my wife, it looked as though she was fading in and out. The nurse checked her vitals and examined her heart monitor, everything read normal. She assured my wife that she was going to be fine, as she also instructed my wife to calm down and take deep breaths.

The whole time I'm with my wife, I was praying. I had an idea where her anxiety came from. You see, the person who hurt her as a child had come up to visit us. This moment was actually about five months after the birth of our first daughter. When the nurse asked her what changes happened in her life, I knew right then and there, that the painful memories of her past were sending her into a bad place. Truth is, this was around the time my wife's cousin called and told her the same person also molested her. This sent my wife into a bad place. I had to be there for her emotionally, physically, and spiritually. I had to be focused in the moment. I had to pay attention to her unspoken cry. Why did she become so emotionally distressed? What sent her to that point?

This was only one of many unspoken cries I had to pay attention to. I can remember coming home finding holes in the wall. My wife would experience emotional breakdowns. Because of the anger and rage developed due to trauma, she would punch holes in the wall. These were some of the scariest times of my life. I had to become present emotionally, have patients, and maintain poise in those moments.

Being present psychologically and emotionally is what I had to do whenever she started experiencing emotional distress. I had to gain an understanding of how to handle these types of situations. I even believe communication is so vital during these times. If you struggle with maintaining effective communication within your marriage, I encourage you to really put more energy in building that part of your relationship with your spouse. Without communication, it's basically impossible for the two of you to move forward into wholeness.

Having effective communication within our marriage, allow my wife to voice what she's feeling. If your significant other is unable to communicate their feelings to you, this can become a real problem. While she's pouring the things that are on her heart, you should always listen to what she is not saying. Men, this is important. You don't want to be the one who misses the unspoken language of her pain. I consider this to be a learned ability. Over time, you learn the things your wife isn't saying. Those things she really wants to express from her heart. Men, listen to her emotions. Hear what her brokenness is saying in the moment.

Sometimes it wasn't easy for my wife to explain or articulate how she was actually feeling. However, whenever I pay close attention and listen with my entire being, I begin to hear her heart. For some of you that know, this is also called active listening. The ability to fully concentrate, understand, and respond to what she's saying and feeling. You begin to hear the fruits produced from her brokenness. This is also known as broken fruit. I will explain what broken fruit is in another chapter.

My wife was really crying out for help from a broken place. I would even say, there were times she was ready to let everything go. I couldn't let that happen. I needed her and we have four beautiful children who needed her. At the end of the day, I was willing to stand and fight with her through every step of her healing process. It was my responsibility as her husband to heal with her.

I remember a time where I started praying randomly in my living room. I didn't know why, but I soon found out why God had me in that posture. Men, It's not enough to be there physically, as mentioned before. You must be present spiritually as well. So, while I'm in my living room praying, my wife was in the bedroom

fighting. Leading up to that point we had a lot going on.

Emotions were everywhere.

She told me later, that the only thing that saved her was

my prayer to God. She literally felt God grab her by the

hand, as she was sinking. She was sinking fast! Her

mind was scattered and she couldn't make sense of her

life. She felt her life moving in a downward spiral. My

wife was ready to give up her last breath.

Now, what if I would've ignored the spiritual attacks,

the mood changes, and the holes in the wall? These

actions

are all considered responses from an unspoken cry.

Once again, I had to learn how to be physically,

emotionally but most of all spiritually present in those

moments. I had to really become focused, in order to

understand her unspoken language.

I found out fast that it wasn't enough to perform in the bedroom. While sex is a beautiful thing, there's still more to it than that. We men often make the mistake of believing, as long as I "sex" her right, she will be okay. Trust me when I say this, that's not the case with a fragile woman, someone who has experienced psychological distress due to trauma.

Matter of fact, sometimes sexing your wife who was sexually assaulted can potentially push her further into a dark place. The thought of having sex could very well send her spiraling out of control. These moments can potentially prevent her from fully healing. Once again, this is another unspoken language you should become aware of.

While we all have sexual needs and desires, I had to make that sacrifice of becoming selfless. Yes, I said what I said and I know this isn't popular. I was sometimes more concerned about my wife getting well, than how I can satisfy my sexual needs. I really wanted to see my wife whole. Trust me, this is easier said than done. Let me tell you why.

There were times where I thought sex was the answer, in order to make my wife feel better. I figured if I could touch that emotional spot sexually, it would calm her down and change her whole mood. I can remember many times after sex, where my wife would curl up into a fetal position. She would begin to cry. Now, I didn't understand it at first. Why would she do that? When it first happened, I thought to myself "yeah I did that, I hit that spot". But I soon found out, that wasn't the case at all. I realized she was responding to the trauma that she experienced as a child, and it was now affecting us in our times of intimacy. I was experiencing the unspoken language of her brokenness.

My wife would even sometimes freeze up in the middle of sex. Now, for some of you, that really understand the importance of having intimacy within your marriage, you can imagine what was beginning to happen in our relationship. Things were beginning to change and I didn't like it. I mean, who really enjoys the feeling of being rejected by your spouse? To be honest, that's another conversation. You don't know rejection until you're ready to make love to your wife just to find out she's not really feeling it. There were times I felt as though I was losing her. If I couldn't make her happy or satisfied in bed, how in the world can I expect the flames of love to increase? This became a major problem for us.

I seriously didn't know how to engage in or initiate sex with my wife. If I touched her a certain type of way, she would shut down. I would sometimes hit her on the butt, hoping I get the response of "I want you", only to get the look of displeasure. I would do it again to see if her reaction would change, only to get an attitude from her. Clearly, she must be disgusted with me. But why? What did I do to deserve this? There was an unspoken cry I had to listen to. I had to understand that language and then make the necessary adjustments. I would be lying if I told you this didn't bother me. Truth is, this messed me up mentally. However, my desire to see my wife walk in wholeness became my focus.

One night, I remember asking my wife, "When did you start enjoying sex?" What she told me shook me to my core. Her response was, "In our seventh year of marriage". She went on to tell of me of times during intimate moments, where she would say to herself, "I wish he would hurry up". Those were some of the nights she would just lay there afterward, as tears roll down her face onto the pillow. This had to be so traumatic and painful for her. I can imagine what was going on in her mind. I knew she had questions because I certainly did. How do we navigate these moments? Also, what does our future look like?

She went on to explain how her pregnancies were the best times for her. She would use her pregnancy to get out of having sex with me. How bad did her trauma really mess her up? I can remember times where I felt like I raped my wife. Not because I forcefully took it from her but because of her body language afterward. During these moments, I really began to understand just how much her childhood traumas damaged her psychologically. My wife was so fragile.

As a man, this really messed with my mind. During intimate moments of our marriage, I had to change my approach. I had to realize that it wasn't about me. Even in bed, I became selfless. I had to pay attention to her body. I had to recognize the triggers. What actions caused her to revisit those painful memories? If I saw or felt her body shutting down, I would immediately lose interest in having sex with her. After all, I didn't want to add to her brokenness or trigger any painful memories of her past. It had gotten to a point that the only time I had sex with her was if she initiated every moment. I was starting to learn and understand her triggers. Once you identify those triggers, you then become responsible for making adjustments. Again, I had to become aware of her unspoken pains.

It had gotten to the point where I couldn't do certain things to her in bed. She would tell me I had to be more creative and think outside the box. She was basically telling me that anything I did in the bedroom, there was a memory attached to it. How do you think I felt when I realized that certain things I did in bed reminded her of someone that caused trauma in her life? This would soon begin to mess with my psyche.

When I developed the awareness of my wife's triggers, I had to make every effort to avoid those actions that could potentially send her down a spiral road. I promise you, this wasn't easy. While we are all imperfect people, you will without question miss those triggers. However, I believe the worse thing you can do is to purposely ignore those triggers for selfish reasons. This was psychologically draining for me. But, I wanted my wife to become whole.

How do I function mentally, knowing that certain things I did, reminded my wife of the people who hurt her? I had to learn and learn fast. I couldn't take it personal. Although my pride wanted to rush her through her healing and wholeness, I had to take my time. I had to be patient! I would say to all my men, don't rush her process. I don't care how impatient you

become. If you love her, and want to see her whole,

you make the necessary adjustments and heal with

her.

Chapter 6

"Broken Fruit"

After my wife explained to me what happened to her, I made up in my mind I wanted to see her live in wholeness. But how do I adjust from having to hear in detail about what took place in her childhood? Truth is, in that moment of her telling me, I had to adjust mentally. I had to learn how to be a husband to my wife. In other words, I couldn't treat her like any other woman I've dated in the past. My pursuit had to be tailored to the success of her complete wholeness.

Understand there are roots created when something so traumatic occurs in your life. If not confronted, those roots have the potential of growing extremely deep into the heart. Also attached to those roots are spirits, which I will talk more about.

Throughout my wife's childhood, it was impossible for her to know what effects these experiences would have on your mind in the future. What would become of those seeds that were planted? It wasn't until she had gotten older and she started to pursue relationships. That's the moment where everything attached to that traumatic experience begins to rise to the surface. People begin to experience her broken fruit. She was beginning to shut down whenever someone would do something that reminded her of the individuals that hurt her in the past. As stated before, traumas can be either physical abuse or verbal abuse. Either way, those seeds eventually rise to the surface, where you then must confront, confess, and release it.

As a seed sprouts up from the ground and produces fruit, seeds planted by painful experiences can also produce emotional fruits. To name some, these fruits can range anywhere from hatred, fear, bitterness, anger, disappointment, resentment, abandonment, and more. I personally had to experience some of these fruits I just mentioned in my marriage.

Let's talk more about broken fruit. I believe it's safe to say we're all familiar with trees and how they provide fruit in the right season. Once a seed is planted in the right environment, the only thing that's really needed for the seed to sprout is the right amount of water, nutrients, and time. Before a tree manifest, the seed has to break. Once the seed is broken, it begins to spout up. One thing about a seed, you can't consume its' fruit until the tree matures. In other words, once the fruits on the tree become ripen, you can then enjoy it.

On the other hand, you may accidentally harvest and consume fruits that are overripe. From an emotional perspective, I call this kind, broken fruit. These fruits are either too ripe to be eaten or have reached beyond what is considered its' best. At this stage of the fruit, it's now beginning to decay. This fruit is no longer considered useful.

Allow me to explain this on an emotional level, as it pertains to where my wife and I were. By now you're aware of the traumas my wife experienced as a child. As mentioned before, seeds were planted the moment she was violated. These seeds would manifest in her adulthood as hatred, bitterness, anger, resentment, and disappointment, just to name a few. Every so often, these broken fruits would appear in our marriage.

I would recognize it the moment my wife's mood started to change. I would even begin to experience these fruits in the bedroom, the taste of over-ripeness. The thing about it, my wife didn't know that she was projecting broken fruit. Let's be honest, when a tree produces fruit, do you ever see a tree harvesting from it's own branches? Absolutely not! I believe the fruits we produce are for others to enjoy. Galatians 5:22 talks about the fruits of the spirit. There's love, joy, peace, longsuffering, gentleness, goodness, faith, meekness, and temperance. These are the types of fruit you should want to produce.

The reality is, whenever someone experiences trauma in their life, instead of positive fruit showing up, you start to show the broken fruit. This is another unspoken language of a fragile woman. You begin to identify the tree by its fruit. What language do her fruits speak? Can you feel the love? Can you taste the joy of her fruit? If not, there's a good chance the wrong seeds were planted in her. You're now experiencing the bitterness of her fruit, the anger of her fruit, and even the doubt of her fruit.

Don't get me wrong my wife also displayed the fruits of the spirits. While we all strive to be more like Christ, we will definitely miss moments to exemplify those fruits. However, some days were better than others. What some of you don't know about my wife is, she has this joy that I can't explain. I would sometimes ask, "Where in the world you get all that joy from?" Especially coming from someone who experienced something so painful in his or her life.

I had to make sure I didn't take what I was harvesting personal. This wasn't easy. I remember opening up to my wife about how she often treated me. She would give me attitudes for no reason. I knew where the attitudes were coming from but that didn't mean I enjoyed being yelled at. My wife would show signs of bitterness towards me, but I knew it wasn't her fault. She was only manifesting the seeds that were planted. I couldn't even touch her and it had gotten to the point where she really couldn't stand me looking at her. I could tell she was battling. I believe in those moments she probably didn't feel beautiful. She might've been disgusted with herself. I'm sure so many emotions were going through her mind.

There were times I would compliment my wife just to show her that I was paying attention to her. It seemed as though it didn't matter what I did or said to her, it wasn't good enough. At one point in our marriage, I started to experience rejection. Maybe I wasn't good enough. This would run through my mind all day while I'm at work, just to come home to attitudes and frustration. Those broken fruits were really pushing me into a bad place. Now, naturally I don't eat every type of fruit, but I enjoy eating fruit that is ripe, you know, the love and peace kind.

Have you ever gone to the store to pick a fruit that appeared to be ripe? That happens to me a lot actually. I'm from Florida and can never pick a good watermelon. My mouth would be watering, just to slice it open to find it overripe. From an emotional point of view, my wife projected exactly what she wanted people to see. You may be attracted to her smile, but there's a story behind it. Her joy might be contagious but there's also a mental battle going on in her mind. If you stay around a broken person long enough, you will begin to see their broken fruit.

I haven't even mentioned the smell of overripe fruit. Some people are pretty skilled at detecting whether or not an actual fruit is overripe. The smell is different from ripened fruit. Just like actual fruit, there's a smell or should I say a certain energy that is released from broken fruit. To be honest, the types of people who are attracted to this kind of fruit are typically broken people. Interesting, right?

Have you ever heard the saying "misery loves company"? This is true on so many levels. I believe certain traumas people have experienced in their life can cause them to connect with people who have experienced similar hurt. As over-ripened fruit attract maggots and fruit flies, your brokenness has a way of attracting people who are not entering your life to help you become whole. More than likely, whatever they're battling or struggling with has become attracted to the energy your trauma is emitting.

I would say in this moment, begin to check your circle. If friends are okay with you living in your brokenness and not trying to challenge you to heal, remove yourself immediately. Trust me, it may hurt but it's so worth it.

By the way, once you disconnect yourself from those types of people, you owe them no explanation. This will make sense when you begin to break away from them and take your healing seriously. As the husband, I had to pay attention to all of this.

There are also spirits attached to childhood and adulthood traumas. Whether or not you acknowledge it, if you haven't gone through deliverance or entered a place of wholeness, more than likely they're still there. This is what my wife and I had to face in our marriage, the projection of broken fruit as well as demonic oppression. Seeds were planted the moment my wife was touched inappropriately in her childhood. Over time, those seeds manifested and opened doors for demonic strongholds. Do you remember "8853"? I told you that God spoke through me and said, "There are doors that are open". While this is considered "spooky" for many people, it doesn't change the validity of my statement that spirits are real!

Just what my wife and I experienced prior to marriage at "8853", once we were married, my wife and I had to personally combat spirits in our home. Let me tell you this, those spirits are nothing like what you've seen in movies. These spirits want to pervert and kill everything God made and designed you to be. That moment back at my apartment was different. That night we only experienced the entire room becoming dark. Once we got married, those spirits began to manifest. What do we do now?

Let me insert here, if you're not spiritually in that place to expel demons, you should definitely get plugged into a church community. I highly recommend being a part of a church that understands spiritual warfare and is willing to fight with you, to overcome demonic oppression. These spirits love to torment people and keep them bound. These spirits are trying to keep you bound to that mental prison I discussed earlier.

My wife and I would encounter moments like "8853" in our marriage. The difference between what we experienced at my old apartment and in our marriage was we had to learn how to command the spirits to leave, in the name of Jesus. Yes, that's the only name that matters! We had to step into a different type of authority. We had to become activated in deliverance. In another chapter, I share some of those times my wife and I had to cast out demons.

To be honest, "8853" was one of the reasons I had to go deeper into my relationship with God. I could no longer play with my relationship with Him. I had to be sure in my faith. There is no way I could've handled these types of experiences in my own strength. I had to rely solely on God to give me the will and strategy to fight alongside my wife. As a God-fearing man, going into marriage, I knew this was bigger than me. "For we wrestle not against flesh and blood," as stated in Ephesians 6:12. It would take a supernatural power to carry my wife and I through this process of healing, deliverance and wholeness.

Chapter 7
"Emotionally Shattered"

One night my wife and I were in the room talking about a trip she had just returned from. She took a trip down to South Carolina to be with her family. From what she told me, she had a great time. The only thing about it was, her body language told me otherwise. We were extremely happy to see each other. We didn't do much talking. Instead, we let our bodies do the talking. I mean, I missed her you know?

While we were having sex, I noticed something was wrong. I immediately got this strange feeling. It was a feeling of uneasiness. As I'm looking at her, I started to see her shut down. In my mind, I'm thinking she's having another moment, the moments she has whenever something I do reminds her of a painful experience. I just knew she was bothered by her past. But in this moment I was confused. I made sure I did everything I could to avoid her triggers. This was different. I've never seen her shut down this early into sex. I couldn't continue.

I stopped and looked at her. Tears started to run down her face. I wiped her tears with my hands and asked her "what happened to you?" When I asked her that, she immediately broke down crying and screaming "why why why?!" Now, my wife is a very strong person. She usually tries her best to keep it together under pressure. This was one of those times she showed just how emotionally shattered she was. But what triggered this moment?

Before I explain to you what pushed her to this point, allow me to expound on what happens when someone becomes emotionally shattered. We are all emotional creatures. We show emotions for different reasons. To only name a few, here are some of the emotions we often expression: happiness, sadness, disgust, fear, and anger. I believe we've all shown at least three out of four emotions listed here.

But what if you're so damaged to the point that even your emotions become broken. What do I mean by this? Just like the analogy I used earlier of something fragile being packaged, what if the item that's in the box becomes crushed or shattered? You realize that someone either dropped the package or it wasn't strapped down or secured properly. At this point, you can no longer use whatever you purchased, for its' intended function. It's now considered useless.

Looking at this example from a psychological perspective, we see how a damaged person began to express broken emotions. Just as I explained broken fruit, you now project shattered emotions on the people around you. In some cases, you end up pushing people out of your life. This happens whenever a broken person becomes emotionally unstable. Truth is, we were designed to show emotions towards each other. I personally believe this is how we really get to know the people who enter our life. How do I know this? You ever encountered someone who shows little to no emotions at all? You're trying to engage with them in conversations but it seems like you're getting nowhere with them. From my experience, this can be frustrating.

I believe God who is also full of emotions designed us to share those emotions with each other. I remember talking to a friend of mine about the character and emotions of God. When God made us by His hands and in His image, every emotion God carried, He also placed it in each and every last one of us. As a matter of fact, with every emotion we share, there's also a certain energy released with it. I'm not going to get too far into that but I hope you get the idea.

Whenever you encounter someone who is emotionally shattered, you can't really enjoy his or her presence like you really want to. Sometimes a person's emotions can shift an entire room. This is the energy I was talking about. For example, my wife has the ability to shift the energy in a room with her presence. When you meet her for the first time, you get this vibrant individual who has so much energy. Her smile alone can light up an entire room.

There were times where my wife would be having a great time but all of a sudden, she shut down for whatever reason. When she shuts down, it's as if someone turned off all the lights in the room. I'm only sharing this to show you just how powerful our emotions are. Your emotions have the ability to really shift someone's entire life. There's also a certain level of influence that comes with the emotions we show to each other. But what if you're emotionally broken? What energy is released then? Can you expect a positive response from the shattered emotions you show towards people?

To connect the bridge, when my wife was crying that night, and asking herself "why", there were so many emotions in that moment. I actually started crying. When we revisited this experience, she told me she could feel my tears dripping on her face as I held her tight. In that moment, we had gone from showing excitement to now weeping because of the memories of her past. My wife breaking downshifted the energy in the entire room. But I wanted to know why?

After I was able to calm her down, she began to explain to me what pushed her to that point. I told you she had just come back from being home with her family. What I didn't tell you was, she had a conversation with one of her cousins who expressed to her that she was also molested. The thing that caused my wife to break down was, her cousin expressed to her that the same person my wife was touched by, also sexually assaulted her.

This shattered my wife emotionally. The whole time she's thinking this individual only touched her inappropriately; he also caused one of her favorite cousins to become fragile. In this moment, more anger and rage was being produced. Things were really beginning to rise to the surface.

How do you really respond when the person you love expresses this type of heartache? This literally broke me. It was important for me not to react in a way that would cause more stress. Instead, I became that shoulder for her to cry on. I didn't have many words to say in that moment. Let us be honest, what can you really say to calm this kind of pain? There's nothing. I had to allow her to go through the grief. At the end of the day, the news she received from her cousin agitated and reopened those wounds. It uncovered her bloody heart. It broke her. The only thing was, I didn't allow her to go through it alone.

Chapter 8
"Handle With Care"

Have you ever watched a video of a delivery person throwing a package at someone's front door out of frustration? This is actually pretty funny to me until it happens to me right? Well, let me explain this to you. Just like that package that was thrown to the ground, this is what happens to women who are damaged by the people they trusted to carry to them. There are people who they thought would never hurt them. Let's be honest, you don't expect a delivery driver to disrespect your product, right? Then why do some people feel it's okay to disrespect the women who trust you to handle them with care?

The misconception is, the handle with care label on a package is only intended for the person delivering the package. Let me help you. That warning label on a box is also meant to warn the purchaser that something fragile is inside. This is one warning label you shouldn't ignore. As mentioned in the chapter "emotionally shattered", you have the potential of damaging the merchandise in the box, if you either drop it or fail to secure the package correctly.

Speaking of dropping packages, how many of you have experienced being dropped before? How did that make you feel? I'm sure the damages caused by the dropping have impacted your life greatly. You can't even love properly. You end up entering relationships with insecurities. You create walls and in some cases boundaries so that nobody would drop you again. Because the people you trusted in your life failed to handle you with care, this has also caused you to even handle others recklessly. If you're not careful, you start to handle the people you connect with just how you were handled in your past. This goes back to the statement I made earlier that broken people hurt people.

Do you really know what happens whenever you experience trauma in your life? Whenever you're mishandled you begin to live through a broken lens. You no longer function the way your original Designer made you to operate as. In other words, it's hard to walk in your true identity whenever something so traumatic happens in your life. You really have to make up in your mind that you are fearfully and wonderfully made by God, as Psalms 139:14 states. In other words, you can't allow your traumas to determine if you're beautiful or not. What did your Designer say about you? What did God say? You really have to trust the process.

Now, from my experience whenever expensive merchandise is damaged during delivery, the company or manufacture either sends you a replacement or you can return it for repairs. I love the bible verse "But now, O Lord, thou art our father; we are the clay, and thou our potter, and we are the work of thy hand" Isaiah 64:8.

Whenever someone in your life damages you, you can go straight to the Father, who is also the potter. You being the clay that was made by His hands, you can also place your brokenness in His hands. He begins to remanufacture you. He cleans up all the fragments and while in His hands, He remakes you. I call this your new beginning. After you leave the potter's hands, you no longer have to look at life from a broken perspective. You no longer have to love with a damaged heart.

Whenever God begins a work in you, have the confidence to know that He will complete that work in and through you. This is how faithful He is. He will not reject your pains. He will not reject your broken heart. Matter of fact, He certainly won't drop you. Once He's finished with you, He produces something better than before. He finds a way to produce glory out of your trauma. The only way for Him to do so, you have to return to the beginning. Return to the place where He first made you, which is in His presence. That place where He blew His breath inside of you. When you commit to the healing process, God will cause you to breathe again.

Once He's finished with you, He delivers you back into the right hands. The hands that will handle you with care. Not only the husband that can handle every part of who you are, but also friends who won't take advantage of the new you. Yes! This is the more attractive you. Not limited to your outward appearance, but this is also your spirit. Perhaps the reason why you can't keep positive people in your life is because of your negative energy or your broken spirit.

Because you were dropped so many times, it caused you to carry an unattractive spirit. When God's finished with you, there will be a glow about you. Your smile will change. Your emotions will change. You will become contagious for the right reasons. The people that enter your life will have no other choice but to handle you with care.

If you're broken, how do you return to the manufacture? I would be wrong not to tell you that the only way is through Christ Jesus. But He's a spirit, right? Let me share this with you. Whenever my wife and I got married, I had no idea that God was going to use me to reach her. It wasn't until I yielded my life to God so that He not only works on me but also through me to touch my wife's broken pieces. Men, if you ever want to know what's your position in your wife's healing process, this is it. Get in position and stay in position. God will begin to show you how to handle your broken wife. He will teach you how to love her with a love that is so different from what she's used to, a love that is not perverted.

My wife was used to being handled a certain type of way that my actions threw her off when we first met. She would wonder why was I so patient with her. Why did I take my time with her? Why did I handle her like a friend she never had? Let me be clear, in no way am I telling you that I was some perfect angle. As I mentioned before, I had my own issues. I was still trying to understand who I was. I still loved my wife from a broken place. But what I want you to understand, even I had to give my brokenness to God.

As He's working and perfecting things in me, He's also reaching through me to work and perfect things in my wife. Men, I really believe the key to your wife's wholeness is you. Yes, you are the key, so kill your pride! Pride will cause you to mishandle your wife.

As she's healing, how you handle her is so important. To be honest, I didn't always get it right. I've handled my wife in ways that could've caused even more damage. Handle her with care? This is seriously easier said than done. This means you have to really become selfless when handling her.

Patience becomes paramount. When God trusted me to carry my wife, I couldn't rush her process. When I committed to the journey to wholeness, I also committed to waiting. Yes, I had to wait for her. I'm not talking about waiting at the altar. At this point, you're already married to her traumas. That's why I believe you have to commit to healing with her. This wholeness is

not only for your wife, but it's also for you.

Chapter 9
"Behind Closed Doors"

I made a statement earlier that broken people do broken things. While it's easy to highlight the brokenness of my wife, let me share with you some of the things I was dealing with. Those internal struggles I was facing. Truth is there were times where I almost lost my wife. Allow me to share some of those times with you. Remember when I told you that on the outside looking in things appeared to be great? Our family and friends would see us laughing and smiling but had no idea what was going on behind the scene. The reality is there were internal doors open.

I considered the third year of our marriage the hardest for me. My wife had just given birth to our oldest daughter. While we showed excitement about our little girl, the truth is the anxiety level was through the roof in our house. I could only imagine what was going on in my wife's mind when she saw our little girl for the first time. I'm sure she wondered if I would ever look at our daughter inappropriately. Will there be a cycle of molestation like she experienced when she was a child? Would I touch our daughter in ways that were only meant for her husband to do when she's married? I'm sure her brokenness was screaming at her.

For the next three years, I would always wonder if my wife ever viewed me as some sick person who would touch our daughter. Did my wife fully trust me? I need you to understand that my wife's perspective and idea of men was perverted. Although we were married, there was still that doubt in the back of her mind. The thing about it, I knew she had those thoughts but I doubt she knew I was aware of what would constantly running through her mind.

I don't care how much good you do. If someone who experienced trauma, such as sexual abuse isn't healed from the pain of that experience, it will affect how he or she views certain things in life. Their reality was sharpened and built upon brokenness. It's built on the backs of disappointment and distrust.

While my wife was struggling with fully trusting me around my daughter, I didn't do a good job of helping her gain trust in me. She was fighting to bring herself past the point of pain, into a place of comfort in her mind. Months after the birth of our daughter, I lost her trust. I would soon see how hard it was not only earning someone's trust but also regaining it. It had gotten to a point where I didn't even trust myself anymore. I realized that I had pushed my wife further into a dark place. Every day from that point forward, I would ask myself "Now what?" Where do we go from here? Is there a future for us?

I know I might've portrayed to be this nice innocent guy, the kind of man that really takes care of his wife. The one who treats his wife with the utmost respect? Right? Wrong! Here's the story.

 I was working the night shift when I decided to message this young lady I was talking to outside of our marriage. Because of our job, we were spending a lot of time together. I was working twelve-hour shifts during this time. This young lady and me had cultivated a relationship outside of work. Now, I can't remember the content of the message this particular night, but I knew it was inappropriate. While I'm messaging this woman, what I didn't know was messages popped up on my iPad screen back home. My wife was home at the time when she just so happened to look down and saw a message notification. She told me that she had gotten a bad feeling when she realized the message was from another woman.

Now, my wife and I respect each other's personal space. We don't usually read each other's messages. My iPad was sitting on the counter in the kitchen when the message came through. It wasn't that she was looking for anything, she was in the kitchen either cleaning or preparing dinner. Long story short, what was being done in the dark had now come to the light.

I need you to understand why this moment was so bad. As I mentioned before, three years into my marriage, my wife was still trying to find full trust in me. Not necessary as her husband, but also as a man. At the end of the day, men were the ones who caused the most pain in her life. If my wife couldn't trust me outside of our home, how can she trust me inside of our home around our daughter? Do you see where I'm going with this?

It's not enough to gain a woman's trust. You have to go to the extent of keeping that trust. How can my wife trust me with her wholeness, if I'm now contributing to her emotional distress? I had just added to her pain. At that moment, I basically pulled the scab from her wounds. For those of you who understand what happens to broken skin once you prematurely remove the scab, you know this was bad. Matter of fact, just think back on a time when you either rubbed against an object by accident and the scab to your injury was removed. I'm sure it started bleeding! The truth is I caused her a lot of pain, on top of what she had already experienced.

This is why your focus as the husband is important. You can't afford to play around with your wife's healing process. You're either going to be all in or not in at all. You can't do both! I lost focus and I was about to lose my wife.

I remember my wife randomly asking me, "Who is she?" There was a short pause before I answered her. Man, the energy that was in the room at the time. I began to feel sweat running down my forehead. For those of you who know about the hot seat, know what I'm talking about. I took a deep breath and said, "It's nothing". What we fail to realize is that it's one thing to entertain other people outside of your marriage but it's another to lie about what's happening in the dark. Truth is she already knew the answer before she asked me. The little trust I once had with her slowly began to drift away. Keep in mind that this is year three of our marriage.

This is why I say trust had to be earned. I find it hard to believe that a person who hops into a relationship start trusting that individual from the jump. There are years of suppressed emotions that will cause them not to trust or even open up to you the right way. It seemed as though my wife was waiting for me to mess up so that she can say, "See, I knew all men are the same". At the end of the day, I was just too good to be true. She found out that I wasn't the man she thought I was, a man who would never hurt her. Someone she could trust with her life and our children's life. Someone who knew how to handle her traumas. That special person who can handle her with care. Things began to take a turn for the worse.

I would then spend the next two to three years trying to regain her trust. To be completely honest, sometimes I feel as though that trust is still shaky. She would sometimes bring up that moment. It would always put me in a place of shame and disappointment. I really had to look deeply at myself. Clearly, there was an underlining issue or reason behind my decision. As I asked God to search my heart, He began to show me exactly what I was dealing with. Truth is I was still battling with lust even in my marriage. The mistake I made was thinking once I got married, it would solve my problem with women. I thought the lust would magically disappear. If you haven't verbally called those hidden things out, nine times out of ten it's still there.

Let me help someone. Just because you marry the love of your life doesn't necessarily mean you now step into freedom. The reality is you still have to confront your demons. There are things we all battled with prior to marriage. To be honest, the fight begins once you enter marriage. You're trying to maintain the purity of your marriage, while at the same time trying to hide what's tormenting you internally. You now have to make sure that the addiction you had prior to marriage doesn't rise to the surface and possibly destroy what you and your wife are building.

I never confronted my issue with lust. Instead, I kept it around. I suppressed what was rooted deeply inside of me. I was addicted to pornography prior to marriage and I brought it into our marriage. First of all, addiction in itself is a stronghold. You can't expect to break addiction in one day and think you're good after that. It's a process. But the thing about it, I never started that process when I got married. I masked what was deeply rooted by showing the world the happy moments of our marriage.

You didn't get the raw images of what was happening behind closed doors. You saw the filtered version of us. You saw the laughter. You saw the smiles. You saw our success. You saw exactly what we wanted our family and friends to see. The truth is we were so broken and so messed up.

Because I didn't deal with the addiction of pornography, every time I looked at a woman to lust, I was feeding that spirit. I was fanning the flames of my deepest desires. These spirits began to hunt me in my dreams. Although I was married, the devil didn't honor it and he didn't care if it destroyed my marriage.

I found myself distancing myself from my wife. That was the worse time for me to even consider shutting down from her. It didn't help that she was still dealing with her traumas. Everything she battled with due to the painful memories of her past was now at the forefront of her mind. She began to shut completely down. She became very angry. She was bitter. My wife was a decision away from possibly causing harm to me.

I'm pretty sure she had just reached her breaking point.

Our marriage wasn't the same. Prior to this moment, whenever I would touch my wife a certain type of way, she would shut down. After things were exposed, she really didn't want anything to do with me. I lost my wife emotionally. As I mentioned to you before, it's important for the man to be there for her both physically and emotionally as well. How can I help my wife walk into wholeness if there's no longer an emotional attachment to her?

Because I never overcame lust, I would pleasure myself in other ways. I didn't know the demonic activity that came along with masturbating. Some may find it harmless but it's not. I promise you the effects of it can destroy your marriage. While my wife is in the bed sleep, I'm in the restroom dishonoring my marriage.

Choosing temporary satisfaction over peace in my house. I wasn't only masturbating but I also brought pornography into our home. Something I refused to deal with before marriage. Do you know what type of spirits I was welcoming into a place that was meant to be our safe space? These spirits weren't only tormenting me but they were now disturbing my wife's sleep.

I will never forget the night I stopped masturbating. The night I said enough was enough! I had just finished doing my thing. After returning to bed and falling asleep, my wife mixing up in her sleep awakened me. My wife was fighting. This fight was different. Do you remember the "8853" story? Right! It was happening all over again. She was spiritually being attacked and was now fighting for her life.

When I saw what was happening, I got out of bed and started praying as if I was the perfect saint. As if I didn't just leave an appointment with myself. The whole time my wife was fighting, I was being convicted. At that moment I knew why she was fighting and I knew what door was opened. We were eventually able to go back to sleep. We made it through the night but I never told her why I felt she was battling so hard.

What we fail to realize is, the things we do in secret don't only affect us but it also affects our family. While you assume what you do is hidden, there are doors you've now opened. These doors would be passageways for demonic attacks. It's important that I highlight the demonic influence that was affecting our marriage. We often dance around the idea of attraction.

I'm sure some of you have heard the statement, "God made women for men to look at". We've gotten to the point where we give spirits a cover name. Instead of lust, we call it attraction. It's harmless, right? Wrong! It's time to call it what it is. You can't expel what you don't expose. It's time to call it out and deal with it. I was battling with the spirit of lust but I never exposed it. Therefore, it remained.

Let me help you. It was only recently where I overcame lust in my marriage. I'm talking seven years into my marriage. One day I was on the phone with a brother of mine. He began to share with me his journey. God was doing a powerful work in his life. He was seeking God like he has never done before. He started to talk about the battle with the spirit of lust and how he overcame the addiction of pornography. I went from smiling with excitement to now being convicted. But why?

It was at that moment where I realized I was still dealing with the spirit of lust. While I was no longer watching pornography, I really never exposed and called out lust. We make the mistake of believing as long as it doesn't flare up, we're good. If you're not careful you will find yourself walking in false deliverance. You will find yourself living in denial. I was only coping with the underlining issue, avoiding the expelling of something that was slowly destroying my marriage. Truth is I was really living in denial because I didn't want to face myself. I didn't want to have to confront that very thing that caused me to inflict pain on my wife.

As I'm talking to my brother and while he's pouring out, something in me started to break. The whole time he had no idea what was happening on my end. While he's talking, I interrupted him and said, "me too". I began to open up to him about my struggle I've suppressed for years. I told him I also struggle with lust.

Understand, my wife and I are doing some great things in the Kingdom of God. We have a ministry called

Awake Worship. Every event God has used us powerfully. I asked him, what sense does it make to do all these good works for the Kingdom but I'm still battling internally? I no longer wanted to be in denial. At that moment I acknowledged my issue and I was ready to release it.

While he's talking, I sent a text to my wife. The text read, "After this conversation, I need you". I told her that the conversation I was engaged in was bringing me through deliverance. I went on to say, "I want to be free!" Once again, you can't release what you don't expose. Sooner or later those things begin to manifest in your marriage. I could no longer allow what was hidden to control me. I confessed what I was battling. Once the light exposes those secret things, do what is best for you and your family and release it.

After the phone call, my wife made her way upstairs. As soon as she made it up there, I started exposing something I had been battling within our marriage. I looked at her and my eyes filled with water. I said, "Bae I want to be free". I began to tell her how I've been battling with lust. I told her that this was the first time where I verbally exposed it. Right at that moment, without hesitation, we begin to pray. God began to show me the lust that was lying dormant inside of me, waiting on the right opportunity to surface.

What I saw in that moment shook me. I saw this big black entity lying in a dark place. While it was lying there, I also smaller entities or should I call them imps. They were constantly going to this black spirit to feed it. This thing was getting bigger and bigger over time. God revealed to me in that moment that this was what's taking place inside of me. Every moment that caused me to lust was feeding whatever was lying dormant.

Understand that the more you feed anything, the bigger it became. This thing was growing and it was waiting to destroy my marriage.

Why am I telling you all of this? This book is about loving a fragile woman, right? How can I love my wife who is broken while still battling something that could potentially cause her more pain? As revealed before, my lust caused me to push her further into a dark place. Because I said, "I do", I made a vow to see my wife live through wholeness. In order for me to contribute to her healing, I had to deal with things I was suppressing. Lust had to go!

Chapter 10
"Confront, Confess, Release"

Throughout this book I've been speaking on demonic influence and oppression, those underlining things that can harm a marriage. Contrary to what some may believe, spirits are indeed real. Growing up, I use to hear my mother say all the time that the devil comes to kill, steal, and destroy. Once I got older I started to understand exactly what she was talking about. It's true. The devil wants to kill you! He wants to steal everything from you. He is trying to destroy you. I wish I could tell you that this journey is easy but that would be a lie. The road to wholeness is a process that many of us try to avoid. Truth is you can't.

My wife and I had to face those things that tormented us in our marriage. As I mentioned before, the moment that door is open, it becomes a passageway for demonic activity. Men, if you want to know how to love a fragile woman, heal first. Expose the things that cause you not to love your wife properly. The thing about it, you can't expect wholeness without freedom from demonic oppression.

My wife and I were inflicted with spirits. The only way to be delivered from these spirits was to confront, confess, and release it. We had to be honest with ourselves. Through honesty, we are able to push into wholeness.

I need you to understand something. You can't expect to expel demons without using the name of Jesus. I know this may not be popular but His name is the only thing that has the power to send spirits running. Matter of fact, the devil trembles by His name alone. My wife and I now know the meaning of James 2:19 "the devils also believe, and tremble". Allow me to share with you exactly what I'm talking about.

Early one morning, my wife woke up fighting. I believe she had just come out of a bad dream. It was around 4:00 am to be exact. When I looked at her, I could tell this moment was different from any other moment we've experienced in our marriage. Matter of fact, this occurred in year seven of our marriage. She began to complain that she didn't feel well. She wasn't sick or anything, she just didn't feel like herself.

While still in bed, I looked at her and immediately knew what time it was. When she turned to me, she stretched her arms towards me and said, "Sam pray for me!" Now, I was able to hear her say my name clearly but the "pray for me" part was distorted. It was as if something else was speaking through her. It started sounding like more of a growl. When I heard it, I immediately went into warfare mode. I started praying in the spirit.

For those of you who know the scripture "we wrestle not against flesh and blood", know exactly what was happening. I can remember the "8853" moment when my small apartment got real dark. This time, these spirits manifested to the point where we had no other choice but to cast it out. We knew it was time to go to war. I asked her was it okay for me to call our bishop at the time and the worship leader? We wanted to make sure our spiritual leader was aware of what was happening. So, I gave him a call but got no answer.

I then called our worship leader, someone we trusted. Besides, she and her family lived down the street from us at the time. In my mind, I'm thinking the more warriors, the better. I began saying to myself, "devil you're in trouble now". Our sister picks up the phone and it's now around 4:30 am. I explained to her what was happening and asked her could she come to the house to assist. Of course, she had to check with her husband but she told me she was on the way. I looked at my wife and told her to put some clothes on. She looked at me, I mean it looked at me and told me "no".

I need you all to understand why I said "it". At this point, I was no longer speaking to my wife. I need to certainly insert something here. Demons know if you have a relationship with God or not. The devil will find out if you've been spending some one on one time in God's presence. Don't allow people to make you believe it doesn't take all of that. Truth is, it takes all of that and more.

This moment was a test of my faith. I've read about times in the bible where Jesus had to cast out demons. One of my favorite scriptures is Luke 11:22, But if you cast out demons by the power of God, then the Kingdom of God has come upon you. This is such a powerful verse for me. I knew that this moment would soon manifest the power of God in our home, and also reveal our authority over demonic oppression. The Kingdom of God was moving in!

I looked at my wife but was speaking directly to the entity that was tormenting her. I said, "I'm not playing with you this morning, now let's go". The whole time this is happening, I'm still praying in the spirit. My wife finally mustered up enough strength to get out of bed and get dressed. Now, the reason I made her get dressed was because I wanted to take her upstairs to our loft. This is our safe space of prayer and worship. If you don't have a room in your house designated solely for the presence of God, I recommend you find a place. I believe this is vital when pursuing wholeness.

My wife is now dressed but she's moving slowly. It was as if she really didn't want to go up there, wait, it didn't want to go up into our loft. The way she explains it, she felt as though she was weighted down. She felt so heavy. When she made it to the stairs that went up into our loft, she clasped. Now, I sent her ahead of me because our worship leader was on the way and I had to make sure I was dressed properly. When I got to the stairs I found my wife crawling up the steps. These spirits were trying to keep her from going up there but my wife found the strength to make it.

Once I made it upstairs, I began praying and calling out things that could've possibly been tormenting her. Understand the names of what was actually oppressing her hadn't been revealed yet. If you haven't encountered anything like this before, I caution you to make sure you're equipped for when the time comes. If you're pursuing healing and deliverance within your marriage, I promise you spirits will manifest. Whether you acknowledge those demonic influences or not, they're still there. Only you can decide if you're ready to be free. My wife was ready to walk in freedom. These spirits were tormenting her for a long time. Enough was enough! Once again, you can't release what you don't expose.

As I'm praying for my wife in the loft, she was also fighting with me. I could feel her pushing and holding on. We had also invited God into the room to fight with us. After about twenty minutes of us warring, our worship leader walks upstairs. She immediately started going in and praying in the spirit. In unity, we all began calling on the name of Jesus. I remember asking the spirits "who are you". If you're experienced in the expelling of demons, you know they will try to trip you up.

They began giving false names. I don't remember any of the fake identities they were trying to go by but I knew it was a lie. As we're praying, my wife began telling us the exact names of the spirits we were dealing with. The moment we all identified what we were battling, we began casting it out in the name of Jesus. We would find out that there were three demons we were up against. We started casting out fear, perversion, and death in the name of Jesus. It had to come out!

Remember when I told you earlier that doors become passageways for demonic activity? The truth is, there were doors still open. If you ever want to know what the process to wholeness looks like, I will tell you it looks like the casting out of spirits. I consider it impossible for someone to walk in total wholeness without total deliverance. I don't care how many books you read, you still must face your own demons, those things that have been tormenting you since the beginning of trauma. I made up in my mind, by any means necessary I must help my wife make it to wholeness. This journey is not for the faint in heart. It takes a lot of prayer, fasting, understanding, and love to reach that point.

This moment was only one of the many times we had to fight. God began to speak to us concerning what took place. He told us that we had just been activated in deliverance. This would be the beginning of my wife and I really stepping into producing atmospheres of deliverance at our Awake Worship events. Because of what took place in the secret place, we wear able to walk people through deliverance in a public place. Understand that this moment in the loft didn't end there. After that morning of warfare, we began unveiling and coming against generations of demonic oppression within our bloodline. Spirits that were passed down because our family decided to stay silent.

What we fail to realize is that silence becomes nothing but an incubator for seeds planted. I believe this is how generational cycles are passed down. No one wants to deal with the shame of traumas. The sad thing about it family members for the longest time have encouraged the generation behind them to keep quiet. There's a fear of the dark secrets bringing shame to the entire family.

What I love about where my wife and I stand right now, I encourage her to expose it. We found out that uncovering and exposing some of the most painful experiences can not only bring you healing but it can also bring deliverance and wholeness to someone else's life. This is what it's all about. At the end of the day, we know that God is able to extract glory out of the most traumatic situations.

Conclusion
"New Beginning"

This journey into wholeness has been trying. Nothing about this road to complete healing was easy, at least not in our own strength. I believe this is seriously a never-ending process. You have to now fight to stay whole. That is why I enjoy my wife's book "Walking In Wholeness". She explains that every single day is a challenge. Our stories are being written daily. You have to make up in your mind that you will not go back to what's familiar. Because my wife is walking in wholeness, we both must walk it out together.

One of the worse things you can do is think you've arrived. To be honest, my wife and I are now walking a new path to maintain this level of freedom. But we chose to take God with us. He's the one guiding our footsteps. When we slip, we will not fall because He will hold us up. We only hope to be an encouragement to every person who reads our stories. While my wife is walking in wholeness, God is teaching every day, how to love a fragile woman.

Don't be discouraged by your scars. I would also add, don't be ashamed of your story. At the end of the day, God will use the broken things to get the glory. Don't remain silent because of what you feel others will say. Silence is only an incubator for the spirit to become stronger. Silence will also cause your traumas to be passed down through to your children. This is why my wife and I decided to share our stories. With boldness and confidence, we say that our brokenness didn't win. We didn't allow what we've experienced to define who we are. We had to rise above the sting of trauma.

As her husband, I had to ask God to show me my identity. This is the only way you can help your wife heal. Men, you must be who God called you to be. Take your place as the protector of her soul. Becoming a protector is not limited to providing physical protection over the house. What benefit is there to provide this type of protection, while your wife is left unprotected spiritually. Yes, a fragile woman is left vulnerable when the man of the household doesn't take his place.

I know this isn't popular. Some may even call this being too deep, but I encourage you to get into the presence of God. He will begin to show you exactly how to love a fragile woman. He will teach you how to handle her with care. Every marriage isn't the same. The way God shows you how to handle your wife will be tailored to her brokenness. This book only gives you my perspective through my experience. That's why it's very important for you to seek God for yourself and your household.

Allow me to explain our new beginning. My wife and I have been on this journey for about eight years. As I'm writing my story, a powerful revelation came to us through a storm that hit our city. The revelation was concerning a new beginning and a new path my wife and I are on.

One night a tropical storm decided to come to our city. The winds were blowing so strongly. It rained all night long. We woke up the next morning to a tree down in our yard. This might not be a big deal to you but let me explain. The night prior to this moment, the Lord spoke to my wife and I. God told us that He was uprooting some things. We were about to step into a new beginning. So, we're standing there looking at this tree in our yard in tears. We truly believe this was symbolic of the new place we are now in. But what really encouraged us was, as we're looking down at this fallen tree, we're looking directly at the roots.

Let me help someone at this moment. Whenever the roots of your trauma become exposed, that is the time for you to confront, confess, and release. Because my wife trusts me with her brokenness, together we were able to confront the spirits that were attached to her pain. Once we confronted the demonic oppression, we were now able to confess the roots that were tied to that traumatic experience. Understand, it wasn't enough to confront and confess, we also had to release every emotion associated with it. We had to release the anger, the frustration, the bitterness, the resentment, the disappointment, the pride, and even the shame.

We are both committed to this process of wholeness. We're taking one day at a time. We won't rush the healing process. We've allowed God to cover us as we both heal. We know that this won't happen overnight. But the most exciting thing about this process is the growth and development. We're stronger because of this. Our love has grown through this. God has definitely expanded and stretched us beyond what we could even imagine. But if I could give you advice, I would say the choice to become whole is yours. Nobody can walk this journey for you. You have to make up in your mind that there's better for you. This can't be the end of your story. There's a better narrative designed and written just for you. Trust the Master's hand and I promise you He will not drop you. No experience will be wasted in Jesus's precious and matchless name, Amen.

About the Author

Samuel Tolbert is the author of Loving a Fragile Woman. He was born in West Palm Beach Florida, and now lives in Hampton Roads Virginia with his beautiful wife and 4 gorgeous children. He's a college graduate who obtained his Bachelors degree and also began pursuing his Master's degree. He's the founder of AWAKE Worship, a platform designed to provoke authentic worship to the Father, through creative arts. He's also the co-founder of Couple Convo, an organization created for married couples, as well as individuals looking to get married some day. He loves the Most High God with all of his heart. Samuel has a passion for marriages. Him and his wife Tre'elle have a powerful story, which they can't wait to share with the world. He believes through their experiences, hope can be restored in marriages and people who are looking to get married some day, learn what conversations to have prior to marriage and during marriage.

Made in the USA
Monee, IL
26 May 2021